MODERN *flowers* ™

Introduction

Barbara Campagna's patterns in this book are designed with a clean, graphic approach in mind—bold floral shapes that are representational and illustrative rather than realistic; they contain contemporary color palettes with very little shading.

Several of the designs feature DMC's new color variations embroidery floss. The use of this thread unveils a succession of color nuances which are unique to each project and add a modern dimension and a delicate aspect to the designs, all in a fraction of time. You'll enjoy adding a touch of fresh blooms to any room of your home with Barbara's crisp, contemporary designs.

Meet the Designer

As a teen, Barbara's passion for drawing and painting turned into a career path, although she continued to enjoy creating handcrafted items. It was during this time that her best friend introduced her to counted cross-stitch. This new medium turned out to be the perfect way to blend Barbara's love of art and craft together. With a handful of colored pencils and a pad of graph paper, she used her drawings to create her first original cross-stitch patterns.

In 2009, with a dozen cross-stitch patterns and a brand-new logo, Barbara opened shop on Etsy.com and Stitch Notions was born. Today, she has over 30 patterns available on Etsy.com, ePatternsCentral.com and AnniesAttic.com.

Barbara studied graphic design, painting and printmaking at the College for Creative Studies in Detroit, Mich., and has worked as a graphic designer in the Metro Detroit area for over two decades. She lives in Troy, Mich., with her husband, Andrew, and their three children. This is her first book of cross-stitch designs.

Contents

4 Field Flowers Wall Art
15 How Does My Garden Grow?
19 Blooming Poppies Accent Pillow
22 Modern Greenery Place Mat
24 Floral Breadcover
26 Blue Posies Towel Border
28 Garden Leaves Pillowcase

Field Flowers Wall Art, **page 4**

How Does My Garden Grow?, **page 15**

*Blooming Poppies
Accent Pillow,*
page 19

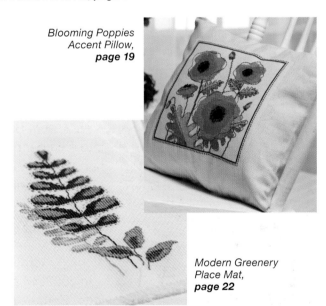

*Modern Greenery
Place Mat,*
page 22

Floral Breadcover, **page 24**

Blue Posies Towel Border, **page 26**

Garden Leaves Pillowcase, **page 28**

House of White Birches, Berne, Indiana 46711   AnniesAttic.com

Field Flowers Wall Art

MATERIALS FOR EACH

- Khaki 28-count
  even-weave cloth:
  8 x 17 inches

Field Flowers Wall Art was stitched on khaki 28-count 100 percent cotton even-weave cloth by MCG Textiles, working over 2 threads using DMC floss. Finished pieces were custom framed.

SKILL LEVEL
Easy

INSTRUCTIONS
Center and stitch design on 28-count even-weave cloth using 2 strands floss for Cross-Stitch and Three-Quarter Cross-Stitch, and 2 or 3 strands floss as indicated in key for Backstitch and Straight Stitch. For Straight Stitch on white flower stems, work over 2 or 3 stitch spaces at a time.

House of White Birches, Berne, Indiana 46711   AnniesAttic.com

Blue Field Flower

STITCH COUNT
61 wide x 199 high

APPROXIMATE
DESIGN SIZE
11-count 5½" x 18"
14-count 4⅜" x 14⅛"
16-count 3¾" x 12⅜"
18-count 3⅜" x 11"
22-count 2¾" x 9"
28-count over 2 threads
    4⅜" x 14⅛"

CROSS-STITCH & THREE-QUARTER CROSS-STITCH (2X)

DMC		ANCHOR	COLORS
White	✳	2	White
727	╱	293	Very light topaz
801	▣	359	Dark coffee brown

DMC COLOR VARIATIONS		COLORS
4010	✦	Winter sky
4215	◆	Northern lights
4220	◉	Lavender fields

BACKSTITCH & STRAIGHT STITCH

DMC		ANCHOR	COLORS
White	▬	2	White* (3 strands—stems of white flowers)
801	▬	359	Dark coffee brown* (3 strands—flower center, petals of blue flowers)

*Duplicate color

House of White Birches, Berne, Indiana 46711 AnniesAttic.com

CROSS-STITCH & THREE-QUARTER CROSS-STITCH (2X)

DMC		ANCHOR	COLORS
White	✳	2	White
727	╱	293	Very light topaz
801	▫	359	Dark coffee brown

DMC COLOR VARIATIONS		COLORS
4010	✦	Winter sky
4215	◆	Northern lights
4220	◉	Lavender fields

BACKSTITCH & STRAIGHT STITCH

DMC		ANCHOR	COLORS
White	▬	2	White* (3 strands—stems of white flowers)
801	▬	359	Dark coffee brown* (3 strands—flower center, petals of blue flowers)

*Duplicate color

Pink Field Flower

STITCH COUNT
66 wide x 199 high

APPROXIMATE DESIGN SIZE
11-count 5⅞" x 18"
14-count 5" x 14¼"
16-count 4¼" x 12½"
18-count 3¾" x 11"
22-count 3⅛" x 9"
28-count over 2 threads
    5" x 14¼"

CROSS-STITCH & THREE-QUARTER CROSS-STITCH (2X)

DMC		ANCHOR	COLORS
White	✳	2	White
727	/	293	Very light topaz
801	▫	359	Dark coffee brown

DMC COLOR VARIATIONS		COLORS
4110	═	Sunrise
4160	✚	Glistening pearl
4190	●	Ocean coral

BACKSTITCH & STRAIGHT STITCH

DMC		ANCHOR	COLORS
White	▬	2	White* (2 strands— outline "petals" on white flowers; 3 strands—stems on white flowers)
801	▬	359	Dark coffee brown* (3 strands—outline centers and petals on pink flowers, stems)

*Duplicate color

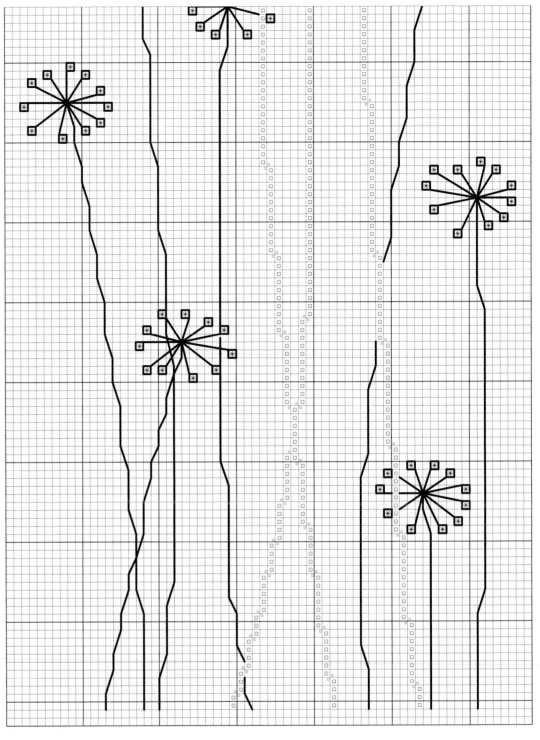

CROSS-STITCH & THREE-QUARTER CROSS-STITCH (2X)

DMC		ANCHOR	COLORS
White	✳	2	White
727	╱	293	Very light topaz
801	▫	359	Dark coffee brown

DMC COLOR

VARIATIONS			COLORS
4110	═		Sunrise
4160	✚		Glistening pearl
4190	●		Ocean coral

BACKSTITCH & STRAIGHT STITCH

DMC		ANCHOR	COLORS
White	▬	2	White* (2 strands— outline "petals" on white flowers; 3 strands—stems on white flowers)
801	▬	359	Dark coffee brown* (3 strands—outline centers and petals on pink flowers, stems)

*Duplicate color

House of White Birches, Berne, Indiana 46711   AnniesAttic.com

Orange Field Flower

ORANGE FIELD FLOWER STITCH COUNT
64 wide x 199 high

APPROXIMATE DESIGN SIZE
11-count 6¼" x 18"
14-count 5" x 14⅛"
16-count 4¼" x 12⅜"
18-count 3⅞" x 11"
22-count 3⅛" x 9"
28-count over 2 threads
   5" x 14⅛"

CROSS-STITCH & THREE-QUARTER CROSS-STITCH (2X)

DMC		ANCHOR	COLORS
White	✳	2	White
727	╱	293	Very light topaz
801	☐	359	Dark coffee brown

DMC COLOR VARIATIONS		COLORS
4090	⌘	Golden oasis
4124	❖	Bonfire
4130	●	Chilean sunset

BACKSTITCH & STRAIGHT STITCH

DMC		ANCHOR	COLORS
White	▬	2	White* (2 strands—outline white flower heads; 3 strands—stems of white flowers)
801	▬	359	Dark coffee brown* (3 strands—centers, petals, pistils and stems of orange flowers)

*Duplicate color

CROSS-STITCH & THREE-QUARTER CROSS-STITCH (2X)

DMC		ANCHOR	COLORS
White	✳	2	White
727	╱	293	Very light topaz
801	☐	359	Dark coffee brown

DMC COLOR VARIATIONS		COLORS
4090	⌘	Golden oasis
4124	❖	Bonfire
4130	●	Chilean sunset

BACKSTITCH & STRAIGHT STITCH

DMC		ANCHOR	COLORS
White	—	2	White* (2 strands—outline white flower heads; 3 strands—stems of white flowers)
801	—	359	Dark coffee brown* (3 strands—
			centers, petals, pistils and stems of orange flowers)

*Duplicate color

House of White Birches, Berne, Indiana 46711   AnniesAttic.com

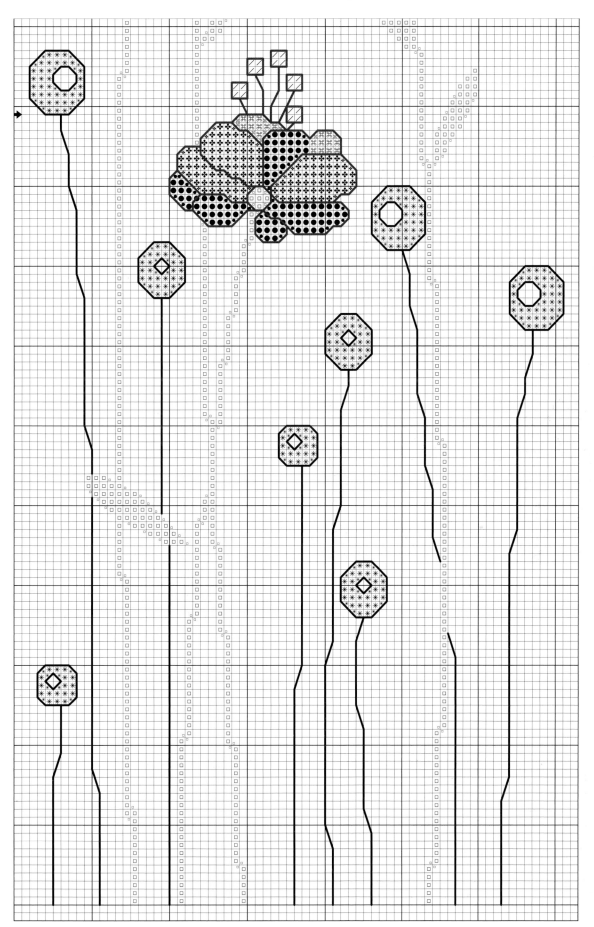

How Does My Garden Grow?

MATERIALS
- White 28-count Aida:
  17 x 13 inches

How Does My Garden Grow? was stitched on white 28-count Monaco cloth by Charles Craft using DMC floss. Finished piece was custom framed.

SKILL LEVEL
Easy

STITCH COUNT
154 wide x 97 high

APPROXIMATE DESIGN SIZE
11-count 14" x 8⅞"
14-count 11" x 6⅞"
16-count 9⅝" x 6⅛"
18-count 8½" x 5⅜"
22-count 7" x 4⅜"
28-count over 2 threads
 11" x 6⅞"

INSTRUCTIONS
Center and stitch design on 28-count Aida, working over 2 threads, using 2 strands floss for Cross-Stitch and Three-Quarter Cross-Stitch, and 2 or 3 strands floss as indicated in key for Backstitch and Straight Stitch.

CROSS-STITCH & THREE-QUARTER CROSS-STITCH (2X)

DMC		ANCHOR	COLORS
347	)	1025	Very dark salmon
353	✳	6	Peach
470	‖	267	Light avocado green
677	#	886	Very light old gold
725	/	305	Topaz
727	O	293	Very light topaz
729	·	890	Medium old gold
730	▲	845	Very dark olive green
733	⊘	280	Medium olive green
742	X	303	Light tangerine
906	+	256	Medium parrot green
907	X	255	Light parrot green
954	■	203	Nile green
991	S	1076	Dark aquamarine
992	⌘	1072	Medium aquamarine
3822	<	295	Light straw
3829	O	901	Very dark old gold
3835	V	98	Medium grape
3844	••	410	Dark bright turquoise
3846	♥	1090	Light bright turquoise
3849	★	1070	Light teal green

DMC COLOR

VARIATIONS			COLOR
4045	◖		Evergreen forest

BACKSTITCH & STRAIGHT STITCH

DMC		ANCHOR	COLORS
353	—	6	Peach* (3 strands—outline center of salmon flower)
730	—	845	Very dark olive green* (3 strands—stems of two olive green leaves)
733	—	280	Medium olive green* (3 strands—center veins of all olive green leaves)
742	—	303	Light tangerine* (2 strands—stamen of blue flowers)
772	—	259	Very light yellow green (3 strands—veins of medium parrot green leaf)
906	—	256	Medium parrot green* (3 strands—veins of light parrot green leaf)
991	—	1076	Dark aquamarine* (2 strands—outline aquamarine leaves)
3819	—	278	Light moss green (3 strands—outline and center veins of Nile green leaves)
3827	—	311	Pale golden brown (3 strands—detail on gold/straw pods)
3829	—	901	Very dark old gold* (3 strands—center of grape flower)
3844	—	410	Dark bright turquoise* (3 strands—petals of turquoise flowers)
3849	—	1070	Light teal green* (3 strands—spokes around center of salmon flower)

*Duplicate color

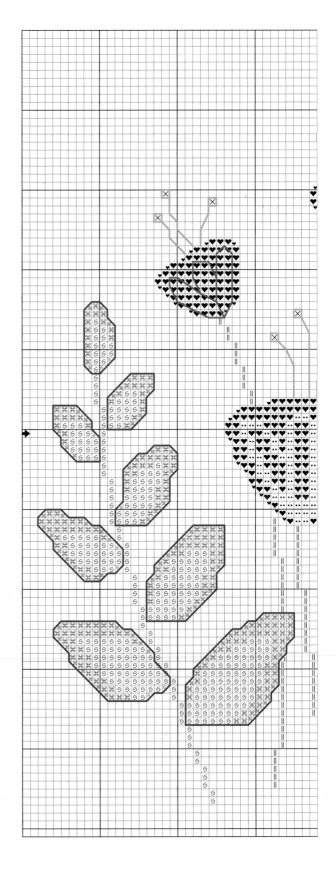

CROSS-STITCH & THREE-QUARTER CROSS-STITCH (2X)

DMC		ANCHOR	COLORS
347	)	1025	Very dark salmon
353	✳	6	Peach
470	‖	267	Light avocado green
677	#	886	Very light old gold
725	/	305	Topaz
727	○	293	Very light topaz
729	·	890	Medium old gold
730	▲	845	Very dark olive green
733	⅔	280	Medium olive green
742	✕	303	Light tangerine
906	+	256	Medium parrot green
907	⊼	255	Light parrot green
954	■	203	Nile green
991	⑤	1076	Dark aquamarine
992	⌘	1072	Medium aquamarine
3822	‹	295	Light straw
3829	◉	901	Very dark old gold
3835	V	98	Medium grape
3844	··	410	Dark bright turquoise
3846	♥	1090	Light bright turquoise
3849	★	1070	Light teal green

DMC COLOR VARIATIONS			COLOR
4045	◖		Evergreen forest

BACKSTITCH & STRAIGHT STITCH

DMC		ANCHOR	COLORS
353	—	6	Peach* (3 strands—outline center of salmon flower)
730	—	845	Very dark olive green* (3 strands—stems of two olive green leaves)
733	—	280	Medium olive green* (3 strands—center veins of all olive green leaves)
742	—	303	Light tangerine* (2 strands—stamen of blue flowers)
772	—	259	Very light yellow green (3 strands—veins of medium parrot green leaf)
906	—	256	Medium parrot green* (3 strands—veins of light parrot green leaf)
991	—	1076	Dark aquamarine* (2 strands—outline aquamarine leaves)
3819	—	278	Light moss green (3 strands—outline and center veins of Nile green leaves)
3827	—	311	Pale golden brown (3 strands—detail on gold/straw pods)
3829	—	901	Very dark old gold* (3 strands—center of grape flower)
3844	—	410	Dark bright turquoise* (3 strands—petals of turquoise flowers)
3849	—	1070	Light teal green* (3 strands—spokes around center of salmon flower)

*Duplicate color

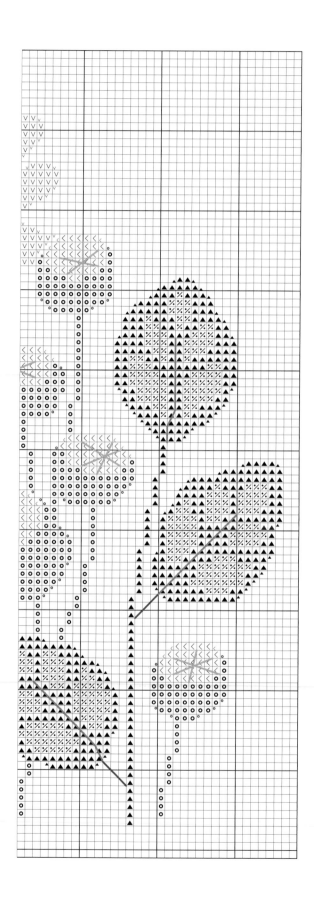

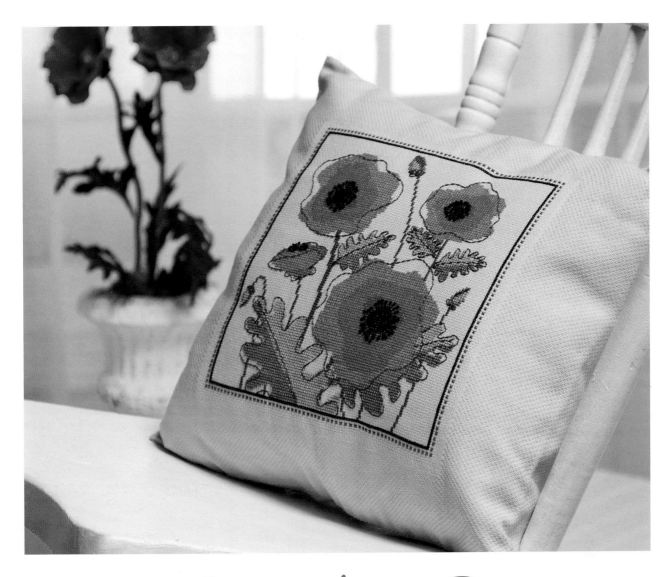

Blooming Poppies Accent Pillow

MATERIALS
- Neutral tea-dyed 15-inch pillow sham with 9-inch-square woven-in 14-count Aida center panel
- 16 x 16-inch pillow insert

Blooming Poppies Accent Pillow was stitched on Home Dec neutral tea-dyed 100 percent cotton pillow sham #PS-2098-6147-EA by Charles Craft using DMC floss.

SKILL LEVEL
Easy

STITCH COUNT
119 wide x 119 high

APPROXIMATE DESIGN SIZE
11-count 10¾" x 10¾"
14-count 8½" x 8½"
16-count 7½" x 7½"
18-count 6⅝" x 6⅝"
22-count 5⅜" x 5⅜"
28-count over 2 threads
   8½" x 8½"

INSTRUCTIONS
1. Center and stitch design on 14-count Aida center panel using 2 strands floss for Cross-Stitch and Three-Quarter Cross-Stitch, 3 strands floss for French Knots (wrapping needle twice), 2 strands floss for Backstitch and 3 strands floss for Straight Stitch working over 2 or 3 stitch spaces at a time.

2. Insert pillow in sham.

House of White Birches, Berne, Indiana 46711   AnniesAttic.com

CROSS-STITCH & THREE-QUARTER CROSS-STITCH (2X)

DMC		ANCHOR	COLORS
310	■	403	Black
321	✳	9046	Red
666	╱	46	Bright red
986	▮	246	Very dark forest green
987	○	244	Dark forest green
989	✗	242	Forest green
3801	═	1098	Very dark melon

BACKSTITCH & STRAIGHT STITCH

DMC		ANCHOR	COLORS
304	—	1006	Medium red (2 strands—outline flower petals, red stitches of top bud)
310	—	403	Black* (3 strands—flower pistil)
986	—	246	Very dark forest green* (3 strands—stamen, detail on both buds)

FRENCH KNOT (3X wrapped twice)

DMC		ANCHOR	COLOR
310	●	403	Black*

*Duplicate color

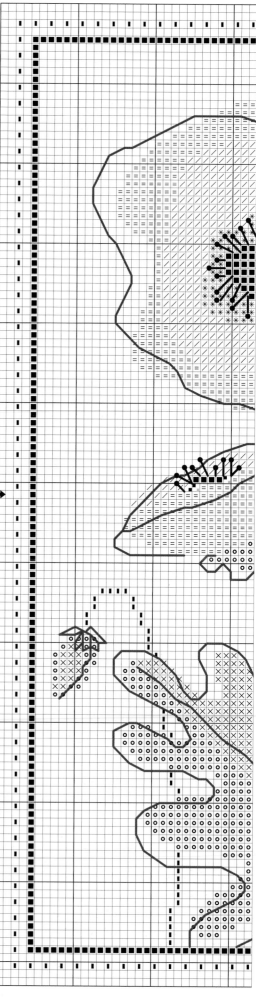

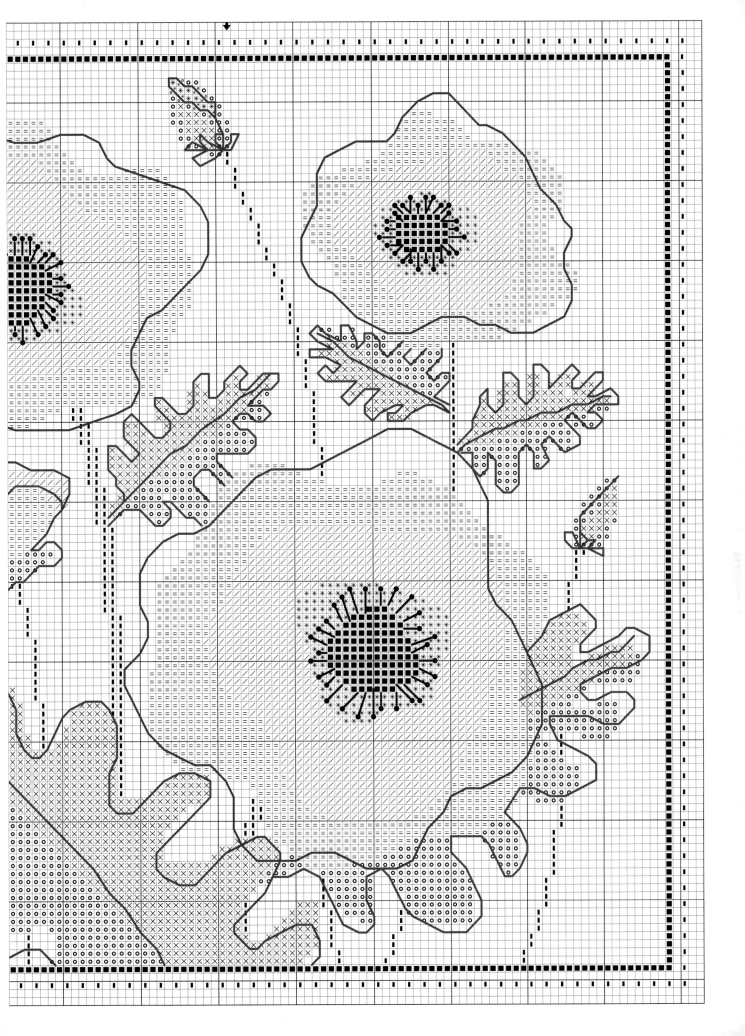

Modern Greenery Place Mat

MATERIALS
- White 14-count Sal-Em Cloth 13 x 19-inch place mat

Modern Greenery Place Mat was stitched on white 14-count 100 percent polyester SalEm cloth place mat with fringed edges #5037 by Crafter's Pride using DMC floss.

SKILL LEVEL
Easy

STITCH COUNT
43 wide x 100 high

APPROXIMATE DESIGN SIZE
11-count 4" x 9"
14-count 3" x 7⅛"
16-count 2⅞" x 6¼"
18-count 2⅜" x 5½"
22-count 1⅞" x 4½"
28-count over 2 threads
    3" x 7⅛"

INSTRUCTIONS
1. Position design in lower right-hand corner of 14-count Sal-Em cloth place mat, approximately 10 spaces from the bottom and 14 spaces from the side.

2. Stitch using 2 strands floss for Cross-Stitch and Three-Quarter Cross-Stitch; use 1, 2 or 3 strands floss as indicated in key for Backstitch and Straight Stitch working over 2 or 3 stitch spaces at a time.

CROSS-STITCH & THREE-QUARTER CROSS-STITCH (2X)

DMC	ANCHOR	COLORS
166	● 279	Medium light moss green
905	△ 257	Dark parrot green
986	⊘ 246	Very dark forest green
989	L 242	Forest green

DMC COLOR VARIATIONS		COLOR
4040	☒	Water lilies

BACKSTITCH & STRAIGHT STITCH

DMC	ANCHOR	COLORS
905	— 257	Dark parrot green* (2 strands—outline moss green leaves, stems)
959	— 186	Medium sea green (2 strands—outline water lilies leaves; 1 strand—stems on water lilies leaves)
986	— 246	Very dark forest green* (3 strands—outline forest green leaves, stems)
3810	— 1066	Dark turquoise (3 strands—broken outline)

*Duplicate color

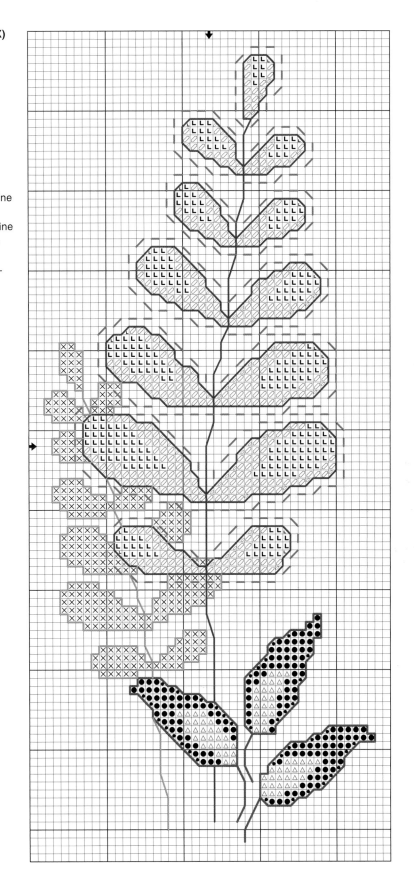

Floral Breadcover

MATERIALS
- White 14-count Sal-Em cloth 18 x 18-inch breadcover

Floral Breadcover was stitched on white 14-count Sal-Em cloth 18 x 18-inch breadcover #5508 by Crafter's Pride using DMC floss.

SKILL LEVEL
Easy

FLOWER STITCH COUNT
53 wide x 53 high

APPROXIMATE DESIGN SIZE
11-count 4⅞" x 4⅞"
14-count 3¾" x 3¾"
16-count 3⅜" x 3⅜"
18-count 3" x 3"
22-count 2½" x 2½"
28-count over 2 threads
  3¾" x 3¾"

LEAF STITCH COUNT
31 wide x 26 high

APPROXIMATE DESIGN SIZE
11-count 2⅞" x 2⅜"
14-count 2¼" x 1⅞"
16-count 2" x 1⅝"
18-count 1¾" x 1½"
22-count 1⅜" x 1⅛"
28-count over 2 threads
  2¼" x 1⅞"

INSTRUCTIONS
1. Position flower design 6 spaces from each edge in one corner of the 14-count Sal-Em cloth breadcover. Position leaf design 6 spaces from each edge in each remaining corner.

2. Stitch using 2 strands floss for Cross-Stitch and Three-Quarter Cross-Stitch; use 1, 2 or 3 strands floss as indicated in key for Backstitch and Straight Stitch working over 2 or 3 stitch spaces at a time, and 3 strands floss for French Knots (wrapping needle twice).

House of White Birches, Berne, Indiana 46711   AnniesAttic.com

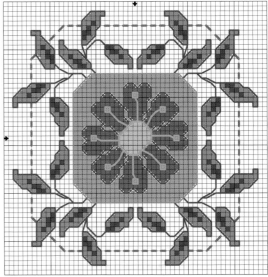

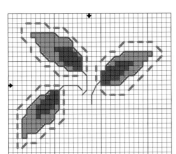

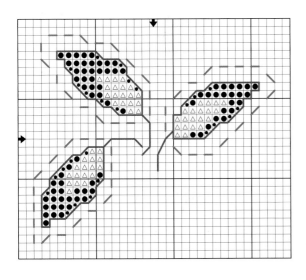

CROSS-STITCH & THREE-QUARTER
CROSS-STITCH (2X)

DMC	ANCHOR	COLORS
166	● 279	Medium light moss green
350	· 11	Medium coral
905	△ 257	Dark parrot green
3855	❘ 311	Light autumn gold

DMC COLOR VARIATIONS	COLOR
4040	✗ Water lilies

BACKSTITCH & STRAIGHT STITCH

DMC	ANCHOR	COLORS
349	— 13	Dark coral (1 strand—outline flower petals)
905	— 257	Dark parrot green* (2 strands—outline leaves, stems)
959	— 186	Medium sea green (1 strand—outline block of water lilies cross-stitches)
3810	— 1066	Dark turquoise (3 strands—broken-line border)
3854	— 313	Medium autumn gold (3 strands—flower center, stamen)

FRENCH KNOT (3X wrapped twice)

DMC	ANCHOR	COLOR
3854	● 313	Medium autumn gold*

*Duplicate color

Blue Posies Towel Border

MATERIALS

- White terry towel with 3-inch-wide 14-count Aida band

Blue Posies Towel Border was stitched on white HomeDec towel #TT-6624-6750-EA by Charles Craft using DMC floss.

SKILL LEVEL

Easy

STITCH COUNT

117 wide x 32 high

APPROXIMATE DESIGN SIZE

11-count 10⅝" x 3"
14-count 8⅜" x 2¼"
16-count 7⅜" x 2"
18-count 6½" x 1¾"
22-count 5⅜" x 1½"
28-count over 2 threads
   8⅜" x 2¼"

INSTRUCTIONS

Center and stitch design on 14-count Aida band using 2 strands floss for Cross-Stitch and Three-Quarter Cross-Stitch; use 2 strands floss for Backstitch and French Knots (wrapping needle twice).

House of White Birches, Berne, Indiana 46711   AnniesAttic.com

CROSS-STITCH & THREE-QUARTER
CROSS-STITCH (2X)

DMC		ANCHOR	COLORS
156	−	118	Medium light blue violet
166	⁄	279	Medium light moss green
351	●	10	Coral
742	✗	303	Light tangerine
3346	⌒	267	Hunter green
3840	✚	117	Light lavender blue
3855	✳	311	Light autumn gold

BACKSTITCH

DMC		ANCHOR	COLOR
351	—	10	Coral* (2 strands—centers, outlines of light tangerine flowers)

FRENCH KNOT (2X wrapped twice)

DMC		ANCHOR	COLOR
3855	●	311	Light autumn gold*

*Duplicate color

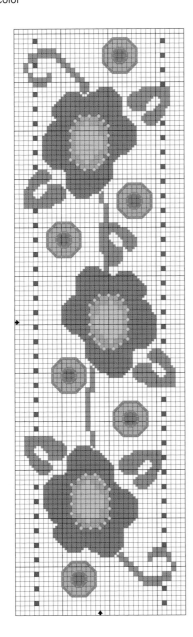

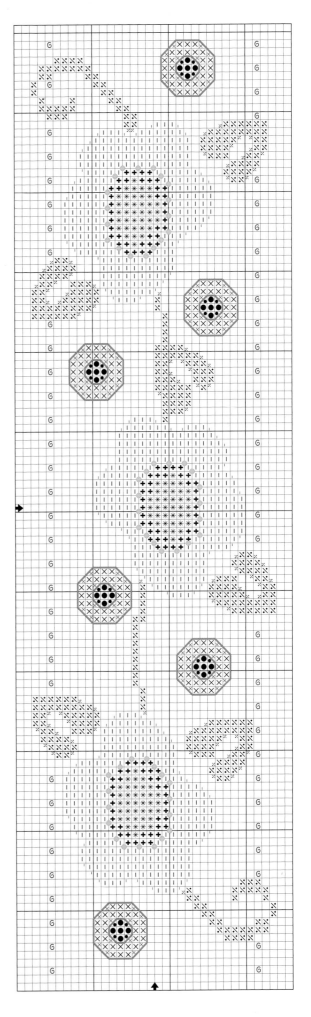

House of White Birches, Berne, Indiana 46711   AnniesAttic.com

MODERN flowers

Garden Leaves Pillowcase

MATERIALS
- White 250-thread count pillowcase
- 14-count waste canvas: 4 x 14 inches

Garden Leaves Pillow Case was stitched on white pillow case using 14-count waste canvas by Charles Craft using DMC floss.

SKILL LEVEL
Easy

STITCH COUNT
34 wide x 165 high

APPROXIMATE DESIGN SIZE
11-count 3" x 15"
14-count 2⅜" x 11¾"
16-count 2⅛" x 10⅜"
18-count 1⅞" x 9⅛"
22-count 1½" x 7½"
28-count over 2 threads
 2⅜" x 11¾"

INSTRUCTIONS
1. Center and stitch design on 14-count waste cloth, following manufacturer's instructions. Use 2 strands floss for Cross-Stitch and Three-Quarter Cross-Stitch; use 2 strands floss for Backstitch and 3 strands floss for Straight Stitch.

2. Remove waste cloth, following manufacturer's instructions.

House of White Birches, Berne, Indiana 46711 AnniesAttic.com

CROSS-STITCH & THREE-QUARTER CROSS-STITCH (2X)

DMC		ANCHOR	COLORS
730	▲	845	Very dark olive green
733	⊠	280	Medium olive green
991	⑤	1076	Dark aquamarine
992	⌘	1072	Light aquamarine

DMC COLOR		
VARIATIONS		COLOR
4050	◖	Roaming pastures

BACKSTITCH & STRAIGHT STITCH

DMC		ANCHOR	COLORS
730	—	845	Very dark olive green* (3 strands—stems of olive green leaves)
733	—	280	Medium olive green* (3 strands—center veins of olive green leaves)
991	—	1076	Dark aquamarine* (2 strands—outline aquamarine leaves)

*Duplicate color

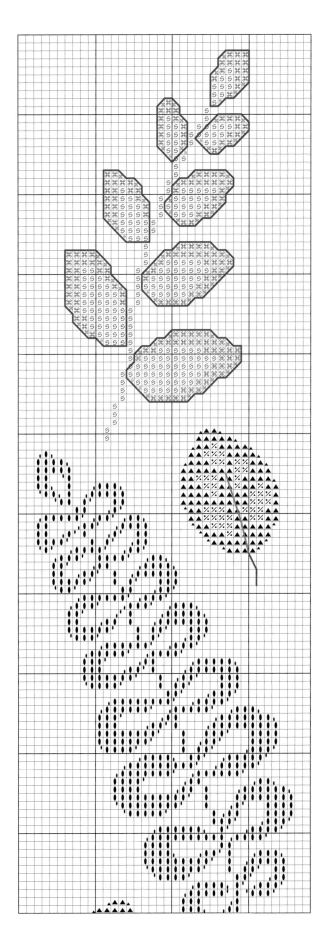

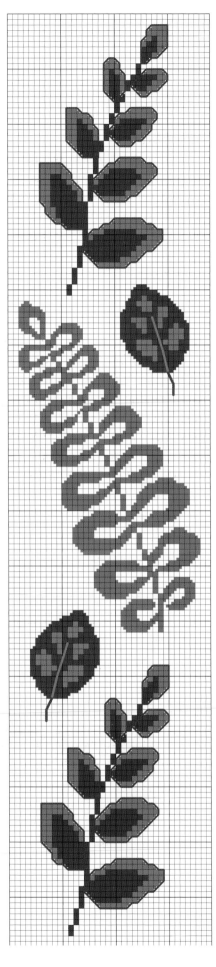

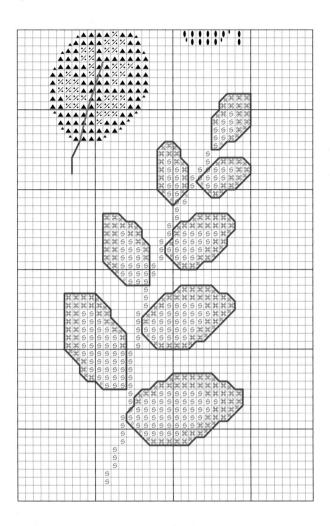

CROSS-STITCH & THREE-QUARTER CROSS-STITCH (2X)

DMC	ANCHOR	COLORS
730	▲ 845	Very dark olive green
733	⅞ 280	Medium olive green
991	𝒮 1076	Dark aquamarine
992	⌘ 1072	Light aquamarine

DMC COLOR		
VARIATIONS		COLOR
4050	◖	Roaming pastures

BACKSTITCH & STRAIGHT STITCH

DMC	ANCHOR	COLORS
730	— 845	Very dark olive green* (3 strands—stems of olive green leaves)
733	— 280	Medium olive green* (3 strands—center veins of olive green leaves)
991	— 1076	Dark aquamarine* (2 strands—outline aquamarine leaves)

*Duplicate color

How to Stitch

Working From Charted Designs

A square on a chart corresponds to a space for a Cross-Stitch on the stitching surface. The symbol in a square shows the floss color to be used for the stitch. The width and height for the design stitch areas are given; centers are shown by arrows. Backstitches and Straight Stitches are shown by straight lines, and French Knots are shown by dots.

Fabrics

Our cover models were worked on 14- and 28-count even-weave fabric that has the same number of horizontal and vertical threads (or blocks of threads) per inch. That number is called the thread count.

The size of the design is determined by the size of the even-weave fabric on which you work. Use the chart below as a guide to determine the finished size of a design on various popular sizes of Aida cloth.

Thread	Number of Stitches in Design				
Count	10	20	30	40	50
11-count	1"	1¾"	2¾"	3⅝"	4½"
14-count	¾"	1⅜"	2⅛"	2⅞"	3⅝"
16-count	⅝"	1¼"	1⅞"	2½"	3⅛"
18-count	½"	1⅛"	1⅝"	2¼"	2¾"
28-count	¾"	1⅜"	2⅛"	2⅞"	3⅝"

(measurements are given to the nearest ⅛")

Needles

A blunt-tipped tapestry needle, size 24 or 26, is used for stitching on 14-count fabrics. The higher the needle number, the smaller the needle. The correct-size needle is easy to thread with the amount of floss required, but is not so large that it will distort the holes in the fabric. The following chart indicates the appropriate-size needle for each size of fabric, along with the suggested number of strands of floss to use.

Fabric	Strands of Floss	Tapestry Needle Size
11-count	3	22 or 24
14-count	2	24 or 26
16-count	2	24, 26 or 28
18-count	2	26 or 28
28-count	2	26 or 28

Floss

Our cover models were stitched with DMC 6-strand embroidery floss. Anchor floss numbers are also listed. The companies have different color ranges, so these are only suggested substitutions. Floss color names are given. Cut floss into comfortable working lengths; we suggest about 18 inches.

Getting Started

To begin in an unstitched area, bring threaded needle from back to front of fabric. Hold an inch of the end against the back, and then hold it in place with your first few stitches. To end threads and begin new ones next to existing stitches, weave through the backs of several stitches.

The Stitches

Use two strands of floss for all Cross-Stitches and Three-Quarter Cross-Stitches; use one, two or three strands for Backstitches and Straight Stitches; use one or three strands for French Knots, as noted in the color key.

Cross-Stitch

The Cross-Stitch is formed in two motions. Follow the numbering in Figure 1 and bring needle up at 1, down at 2, up at 3, down at 4, to complete the stitch. Work horizontal rows of stitches (Figure 2) wherever possible. Bring thread up at 1, work half of each stitch across the row, and then complete the stitches on your return.

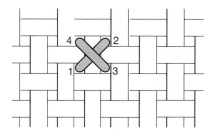

Figure 1

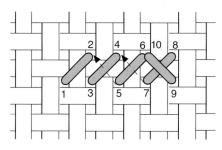

Figure 2

House of White Birches, Berne, Indiana 46711 AnniesAttic.com

Three-Quarter Cross-Stitch

The Three-Quarter Cross-Stitch is also formed in two motions. Follow the numbering in Figure 3 and bring needle up at 1 and down at 2, up at 3, down at 4 to complete the stitch. The Three-Quarter Cross-Stitch is used to fill in spaces in the design where there is not enough room for a full stitch.

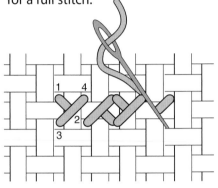

Figure 3

Backstitch

Backstitches are worked after Cross-Stitches have been completed. They may slope in any direction and are occasionally worked over more than one square of fabric. Figure 4 shows the progression of several stitches; bring thread up at odd numbers and down at even numbers. Frequently, you must choose where to end one Backstitch color and begin the next color. Choose the object that should appear closest to you. Backstitch around that shape with the appropriate color, and then Backstitch the areas behind it with adjacent color(s).

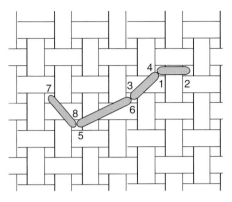

Figure 4

Straight Stitch

A Straight Stitch, Figure 5, is made like a long backstitch. Come up at one end of the stitch and down at the other. The length and direction of these stitches will vary—follow the chart for exact placement working over 2 or 3 stitch spaces at a time.

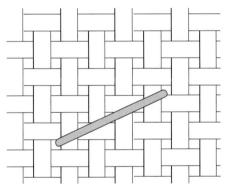

Figure 5

French Knot

Bring thread up where indicated on chart. Wrap floss twice around needle (Figure 6) and reinsert needle at 2, close to 1, but at least one fabric thread away from it. Hold wrapping thread tightly and pull needle through, letting thread go just as knot is formed. For a larger knot, use more strands of floss.

Figure 6

Planning a Project

If you are working on a piece of fabric, determine the stitched size, and then allow enough additional fabric around the design, plus 3 inches more on each side for use in finishing and mounting.

Cut your fabric exactly true, right along the holes of the fabric. Some raveling may occur as you handle the fabric. To minimize raveling along the raw edges, use an overcast basting stitch, machine zigzag stitch or masking tape, which you can cut away when you are finished.

Finishing Needlework

When you have finished stitching, dampen your embroidery (or, if soiled, wash in lukewarm mild soapsuds and rinse well). Roll in a towel to remove excess moisture. Place facedown on a dry towel or padded surface, and press carefully until dry and smooth. Make sure all thread ends are well anchored and clipped closely. Proceed with desired finishing.

HOUSE of WHITE BIRCHES
PUBLISHERS SINCE 1947

Modern Flowers is published by DRG, 306 East Parr Road, Berne, IN 46711. Printed in USA. Copyright © 2011 DRG. All rights reserved. This publication may not be reproduced in part or in whole without written permission from the publisher.

RETAIL STORES: If you would like to carry this pattern book or any other DRG publications, visit DRGwholesale.com

Every effort has been made to ensure that the instructions in this publication are complete and accurate. We cannot, however, take responsibility for human error, typographical mistakes or variations in individual work. Please visit AnniesCustomerCare.com to check for pattern updates.

ISBN: 978-1-59217-347-1

1 2 3 4 5 6 7 8 9